A Colorful Past
A Coloring Book of Church History through the Centuries

by William Boekestein

illustrated by Naomi Kamphuis

Reformation Heritage Books
Grand Rapids, Michigan

A Colorful Past
© 2018 by William Boekestein

Reformation Heritage Books
2965 Leonard St. NE
Grand Rapids, MI 49525
616-977-0889
orders@heritagebooks.org
www.heritagebooks.org

Printed in the United States of America
18 19 20 21 22 23/10 9 8 7 6 5 4 3 2 1

ISBN 978-1-60178-639-5

For additional Reformed literature, request a free book list from Reformation Heritage Books at the above regular or email address.

To Chaz,
a dear friend
and true investor
in the kingdom of heaven
—WB

To my grandpa, Howard Jolman,
whose faith, creativity, and love of beauty
have always inspired me.
—NK

Contents

Introduction

The history of the church has been a tremendously colorful story. In the early days of the New Testament church, Jesus handpicked a dozen ordinary men to be His disciples, students who would learn from Him what it meant to live in God's kingdom. Luke tells us that in just a few years the disciples numbered about 120 people (Acts 1:15). On a single day, a few weeks later, three thousand more believers were added to that number (2:41). From then on, "the Lord added to the church daily such as should be saved" (2:47). Within a very short time the enemies of the church—living fifteen hundred miles away from where Christianity started—could say that the Christian faith had "turned the world upside down" (17:6). And all this happened within a single generation of the death of our Savior!

Since that time God has grown the Christian community into a family of people estimated today at over two billion! Since the beginning, God has raised up men and women to teach, defend, and live out the truths of the Christian faith. The gospel has reached into almost every imaginable part of the world. People of remarkably diverse cultures, skin colors, and levels of education and wealth have come to know Jesus as Lord. Ever since the beginning, men and women and boys and girls have called on the name of the Lord in their own unique language and have worshiped Him according to the instructions of Scripture, though with surprising variety. If we picture the church as a beautiful painting, it is hard to imagine a color that has been absent from the Master Painter's palette.

But this colorful history has not always been happy. Many believers have proved Paul's words: "We must through much tribulation enter into the kingdom of God" (Acts 14:22). Sometimes members of the church have not followed the pattern of godliness Christ has left us. Within the church there has been widespread forgetfulness of Scripture, false teaching, and terrible hypocrisy. But through all the ups and downs, the story of the church has been God's story.

Because of God's amazing power and goodness, the brightest color in the story of the church—shining against the dark background of sin—has been God's powerful grace and His promise to build His church. Knowing this is incredibly important. One of the ways we learn to depend on God's care in our day is to notice how He has always cared for His people despite their tremendous weakness. In fact, the darkest days of church history teach us that the very existence of the church is a miracle.

This coloring book is designed to introduce to children (and their older friends and family members) some of the important characters of church history, focusing on at least one person per century. This method leaves out dozens of important people (there are no unimportant people in God's church). But, hopefully, the use of this basic timeline will illustrate how God has woven these deeply flawed characters, and many more like them, into a single living story. And this story is not over. By coloring these pages and reflecting on the words, children might better see themselves as part of God's story.

The book is designed with an image on only one side of each sheet so that the pages can be removed and transformed into a personalized timeline for classrooms or homes. The "century stamp" helps easily indicate at what point in the church's colorful story each character lived. May the Lord use this book to help us heed the call of Psalm 78:

> Let children hear the mighty deeds which God performed of old,
> Which in our younger years we saw and which our fathers told.
> He bids us make His glories known, the works of power and grace,
> That we convey His wonders down through every rising race.
>
> Our lips shall tell them to our sons, and they again to theirs;
> And generations yet unborn must teach them to their heirs;
> Thus shall they learn, in God alone their hope securely stands;
> That they may not forget His works, but honor His commands.

During the first century AD, Jesus lived, died, was raised from the dead, and returned to heaven. He told **Paul** (c. 5 – c. 67) and other disciples to teach the gospel—sinners who trust in Jesus gain eternal life and forgiveness of sins.

The first disciples trained others to teach the good news. **Ignatius** (c. 35 – c. 108) was a church leader of Antioch, an important early Christian community. Ignatius was thrown to wild beasts to be killed for his faith.

Polycarp (69–156) was another early church leader who communicated by letter with Ignatius. He was the bishop of the church of Smyrna (see Rev. 1:11; 2:8), a student of the apostle John, and a martyr who died for his faith in Jesus.

2ND CENTURY

In the days of the early church, few people knew the true God. God used apologists—defenders of the faith—like **Justin Martyr** (c. 100 – c. 165) to answer the pagan world's hard questions about Christianity. Justin died by being beheaded in Rome.

The young church often struggled to understand the Bible. God raised up **Tertullian** (160–220), a married priest, to help the church begin to grasp doctrines like the Trinity. God the Father, God the Son, and God the Holy Spirit are one.

The young church gained relief from Roman persecution when **Emperor Constantine** (c. 272–337) converted to Christianity. Constantine also called an important church meeting at Nicea (325), which confirmed the Bible's teaching that Jesus is fully God and fully man.

Some early Christians were confused about how Jesus was related to God the Father. **Athanasius** (c. 297 – 373), sometimes feeling as though he was against the whole world, helped show that Jesus was of the same substance as the Father.

Many early church leaders, like **Augustine** (354–430), were African. After becoming a Christian through the prayers of his mother, **Monica** (322–387), Augustine taught that people are thoroughly infected by sin and healed only by God's powerful grace.

Patrick (c. 380 – c. 460) was a British missionary to Ireland, the land where he had been enslaved for several years after being kidnapped by Irish pirates. Through his preaching, many Irish people converted to Christ.

In the Middle Ages, most Europeans had never heard the gospel. **Columba** (521 – 597), a traveling Irish missionary to Scotland, wrote, "I walk secure and blessed in every clime or coast, in the name of God the Father, and Son, and Holy Ghost." The day before he died he copied Psalm 34:10, "They that seek the LORD shall not want any good thing."

As Christianity spread, the church at Rome and her bishop became more powerful than the other churches and bishops. As bishop of Rome, **Gregory the Great** (c. 540 – 604) put much energy into missions, church singing, and education. He also taught, in a simple way, the doctrines of Augustine, though sometimes he was not as careful and as committed to Scripture as Augustine was.

The missionary **Boniface** (675 – 754) preached to the superstitious folk of ancient Germania. Once, to show that there is only one true God, he chopped down a sacred tree and built a church from its wood.

In the Middle Ages, many small tribes and kingdoms became Christian. **Charlemagne** (742 – 814), also known as Charles the Great, united much of the old Roman Empire under one religious kingdom, the Holy Roman Empire. Regrettably, Charlemagne retained a reputation for adultery and forced conversions throughout much of his life.

By reading Scripture (and Augustine), the monk **Gottschalk** (c. 805 – c. 868) reminded the church of two truths: God controls all things, including the salvation of some and the condemnation of others (Rom. 9:18); and Christ died only for His chosen ones (John 17:9–10). Gottschalk died for his beliefs in prison.

As a young prince, **Vladimir of Kiev** (c. 958 – 1015) lived for pleasure and tried to force his subjects to follow old pagan rituals. After becoming a Christian, he removed pagan gods and helped missionaries spread the Christian faith among the Russian people.

CUR DEUS
HOMO

WHY GOD BECAME
A
MAN

As Christianity spread, religious teachers continued to help the church understand the Bible. **Anselm of Canterbury** (c. 1033 – 1109) helped show how Jesus alone, as God and man, could endure on behalf of sinners God's penalty for sin.

Some early Christians followed Jesus by living in monasteries, or religious communities. **Bernard of Clairvaux** (1090 – 1153) was a French monk who preached in favor of the Crusades. He taught the church to sing, "What thou, my Lord, hast suffered was all for sinners' gain."

By giving his wealth to the poor and studying, practicing, and teaching the Bible, **Peter Waldo** (c. 1140 – 1217) tried to live out a religion pure and undefiled (James 1:27). Waldo's followers, called the Waldenses, helped prepare the way for the Reformation of the sixteenth century.

For centuries, higher Christian education took place in church schools and monasteries. With the rise of the universities, scholars like **Thomas Aquinas** (c. 1225 – 1274) worked to explain the mysteries of the faith and to defend it against critics.

As the church refined its teaching, **John Wycliffe** (c. 1324 – 1384) and others began to question the authority of the pope, or the bishop of Rome, and other doctrines that the church valued. Wycliffe helped translate the Bible into English.

John Hus (c. 1369 – 1415) was a popular preacher who had been influenced by the teachings of Wycliffe. Hus ignored the pope's order that he stop preaching. He was cast out of the church and eventually burned at the stake.

During the Renaissance period—the rebirth of ancient learning—Bible teaching and local revivals became increasingly common. The fiery Italian preacher **Girolamo Savonarola** (1452–1498) once led the people of Florence in burning a giant tower of books and other materials that seemed to go against biblical morals.

Some great Christian thinkers, like the Dutchman **Desiderius Erasmus**, (1466 – 1536) agreed that the church needed to reform, but they refused to break with the Roman Catholic Church. Erasmus published an important Greek text of the New Testament that helped produce the King James Version of the Bible.

By the early 1500s, God had prepared the church to return to Scripture. Reformers, like **Martin Luther** (1483 – 1546), challenged the authority of the pope and practices such as the purchase of indulgences—pledges by the pope to soften the penalty of a person's sin. A Reformation of godliness had begun!

16TH CENTURY

While Luther was challenging the Roman Catholic Church in Germany, a priest named **Ulrich Zwingli** (1484 – 1531) was preaching the gospel of God's free grace in Switzerland. The conflict between Roman Catholics and Protestants—those who protested the unbiblical positions of the Roman Catholic Church—led to a civil war in Switzerland in which Zwingli was killed.

The Reformation came to England partly through the work of the first Protestant archbishop of Canterbury, **Thomas Cranmer** (1489 – 1556). Cranmer helped England separate from the Roman Catholic Church. After the deaths of his supporters, King Henry VIII and Edward VI, Cranmer was burned to death by the new Roman Catholic queen, "Bloody" Mary I.

Roman Catholic resistance to the Reformation was especially powerful in Italy. **Peter Martyr Vermigli** (1499 – 1562) was an excellent teacher of Christ who fled Italy because of his unpopular convictions. While he was teaching in England, he became dear friends with Cranmer but fled the country just before Cranmer was executed.

THE TRUE GOD ALONE IS TO BE ADORED AND WORSHIPPED. THIS HONOR WE IMPART TO NONE OTHER.

After the early years of the Reformation, God used later Reformers, like **Heinrich Bullinger** (1504 – 1575), to teach true Christianity to members of the new Reformed churches. Bullinger followed an ancient church custom, summarizing the faith in the Second Helvetic (or Swiss) Confession, a document that is still used today.

John Calvin (1509 – 1564) is one of the most famous of the Reformers. He listened to what others were teaching and read what the church fathers had said and wrote a brilliant guide to the Christian faith, *The Institutes of the Christian Religion*. He also preached, taught, or wrote encouraging letters to other believers almost every day of his adult life.

After pastoring churches in England during the days of Edward VI and in Geneva during the days of Calvin, **John Knox** (c. 1514 – 1572) returned to his native Scotland, where he helped write the Scottish Confession of Faith and helped establish the Protestant faith as the national religion. It was said that Knox "never feared the face of man."

On his deathbed, the young English king Edward VI named his godly cousin **Lady Jane Grey** (1537 – 1554) as his heir. After Edward died, the people turned against Jane in favor of Edward's Roman Catholic half sister, Mary I. When Mary became queen, she unfairly executed Jane for treason. Before dying, Jane read Psalm 51 and prayed for God to receive her spirit.

In his youth **William Perkins** (1558 – 1602) was wild and wicked. After he was converted to Christ and became a minister, he would often preach powerful messages to those whose wickedness had led them to jail. Perkins was one of the first English Christians to be known as a Puritan; he longed for a purified church.

The church that God had begun to reform needed new leaders to teach the amazing message that God saves sinners! **John Owen** (1616 – 1683), another Puritan, masterfully preached, taught, and wrote about the Christian faith. His audience included powerful men, like military leader Oliver Cromwell and King Charles II.

During the reign of Charles II, many Puritan ministers were either imprisoned or forced to quit preaching in the official church, the Church of England. **John Bunyan** (1628 – 1688) was an untrained preacher who, while in prison, wrote *The Pilgrim's Progress*, a parable about the journey of a believer to heaven.

Matthew Henry (1662–1714) was born two months after his father, a Presbyterian minister, was forced to stop preaching. As a child Matthew learned from his father Latin, Greek, and Hebrew. Later, his knowledge of Scripture—in English and the older languages—and his gift of teaching allowed him to write a beloved commentary on the whole Bible.

By the time of the Reformation, Christianity had come to the New World of North America. But, as in the Old World, religion was some-times just a heartless habit. God used preachers like **Jonathan Edwards** (1703–1758)—and his famous sermon, "Sinners in the Hands of an Angry God," based on Deuteronomy 32:35—to cause a Great Awakening of godliness.

After the Reformation, many people who claimed to be Christians failed to live as new creations because they hardly ever heard the gospel preached clearly and powerfully. Traveling preachers, like **George Whitefield** (1714 – 1770), preached to thousands, sometimes in the open air, calling them to return to Christ.

As world travel increased, more Christians came to realize just how many people did not yet know Christ or even have a Bible that could tell them about God's salvation. As the "Father of Modern Missions," **William Carey** (1761 – 1834) helped to translate the Bible into twenty-six Indian languages and introduced Scripture to more than three hundred million people.

Charles Spurgeon (1834 – 1892) was converted to Christ when he was fifteen. That same year he began preaching the gospel. By the time of his death, he had preached many thousands of sermons about Jesus, the righteousness of God and the friend of sinners.

The Christian faith has never needed the support of political power. But throughout the ages God has used people in government to speak and work for His truth. **Abraham Kuyper** (1837 – 1920) was a Reformed minister and prime minister of the Netherlands. He reminded the church of God's absolute rule over every inch of creation.

Christ died - that is history.
Christ died for our sins -
that is doctrine.

God has always raised up people to teach truth and correct errors in the church. In a day when it was popular to deny Scripture as the living, active, and powerful word of God, **J. Gresham Machen** (1881 – 1937) defended the truth of God's living word and worked hard to train up new ministers and missionaries to proclaim the gospel.